M000165240

TODAY
I LEARNED
VOLUME 2

© 2023 Willow Creek Press

All Rights Reserved. No part of this book may be reproduced or transmitted in any form by any means, electronic or mechanical, including photocopying, recording, or by any information storage and retrieval system, without written permission from the publisher.

Published by Willow Creek Press, Inc.
P.O. Box 147, Minocqua, Wisconsin 54548

Printed in the United States

TODAY
I LEARNED
VOLUME 2

**OVER 300 NEW STRANGE-BUT-TRUE FACTS
THAT YOU PROBABLY DIDN'T KNOW.**

WILLOW CREEK PRESS®

WE SHAKE HANDS TO SHOW WE'RE UNARMED.

The origins of the handshake have been traced to medieval Europe, when knights extended their hand to show they were unarmed. The greeting was popularized by the Quakers who embraced it as a more egalitarian alternative to a bow.

FREELANCERS ORIGINALLY REFERRED TO SELF-EMPLOYED, SWORD-WIELDING MERCENARIES: LITERALLY "FREE LANCERS."

THE FIRST TV COMMERCIAL AIRED ON JULY 1, 1941. IT WAS AN AD FOR BULOVA WATCHES.

BLUE WHALES EAT HALF A MILLION CALORIES IN ONE MOUTHFUL.

BABY PORCUPINES ARE CALLED "PORCUPETTES."

THE U.S. GOVERNMENT SAVED EVERY PUBLIC TWEET FROM 2006 THROUGH 2017.

SLOTHS HAVE MORE NECK BONES THAN GIRAFFES.

Despite physical length, there are more bones in the neck of a sloth than that of a giraffe. There are seven vertebrae in the neck of giraffes, and in most mammals, but there are ten in a sloth.

AN ESPRESSO MAKER WAS SENT INTO SPACE IN 2015.

THERE IS A BORING, OREGON AND A DULL, SCOTLAND. THEY HAVE BEEN SISTER CITIES SINCE 2012.

BEETHOVEN NEVER KNEW HOW TO MULTIPLY OR DIVIDE.

170–YEAR–OLD BOTTLES OF CHAMPAGNE WERE FOUND AT THE BOTTOM OF THE BALTIC SEA.

HUMANS HAVE JUMPED FARTHER THAN HORSES IN THE OLYMPICS.

THE SEVERED HEAD OF A SEA SLUG CAN GROW A WHOLE NEW BODY.

Two species of sea slugs can pop off their heads and regrow their entire bodies from the noggin down, scientists in Japan recently discovered. This incredible feat of regeneration can be achieved in just a couple of weeks and is absolutely mind-blowing.

MANY LIPSTICKS CONTAIN FISH SCALES.

Most lipstick contains the byproduct of fish scales, called pearl essence or pearlescence—as it turns out, the stuff that makes fish scales flash also makes one's lips shiny. Most pearl essence comes from commercially fished herring. Synthetic versions are available, but they are not widely used.

CORN WILL ALWAYS HAVE AN EVEN NUMBER OF ROWS ON EACH COB.

NO NUMBER BEFORE 1,000 CONTAINS THE LETTER A.

THE MGM LION ROAR IS TRADEMARKED.

APPLESAUCE WAS THE FIRST FOOD EATEN IN SPACE.

THERE WERE ACTIVE VOLCANOES ON THE MOON WHEN DINOSAURS WERE ALIVE.

FROGS NEVER DRINK.

Frogs do not drink like we do; they absorb water directly through their skin in an area known as the "drinking patch" located on their belly and the underside of their thighs.

PAYPAL ACCIDENTALLY CREDITED A MAN WITH 92 QUADRILLION DOLLARS.

VENUS IS THE ONLY PLANET TO SPIN CLOCKWISE.

YOU CAN RUN FOR PRESIDENT WHILE IN PRISON.

THERE ARE PARTS OF AFRICA IN ALL FOUR HEMISPHERES.

AMERICANS HAVE INVADED CANADA TWICE. IN 1775 AND 1812. THEY LOST BOTH TIMES.

WALRUSES CAN GO WITHOUT SLEEP FOR 84 HOURS.

A MERMAID "DOCUMENTARY" ONCE FOOLED SO MANY PEOPLE THAT THE U.S. GOVERNMENT HAD TO ISSUE A STATEMENT.

In 2013, Animal Planet aired a mockumentary that "proved" the half-human, half-fish beings exist. And while the program was fake, plenty of viewers believed that the fictional claims were real. In fact, so many people were fooled that the U.S. government's National Oceanic and Atmospheric Administration had to release a statement saying, "No evidence of aquatic humanoids has ever been found."

A HOUSEFLY HUMS IN THE KEY OF F.

The common housefly, although it lacks vocal cords, hums by flapping its wings about 190 times per second. We don't hear the individual flaps, but a low-level humming noise in the key of F major.

THE AVERAGE DOG CAN UNDERSTAND OVER 150 WORDS.

WATER MAKES DIFFERENT POURING SOUNDS DEPENDING ON ITS TEMPERATURE.

RHODE ISLAND MIGHT BE THE SMALLEST STATE IN TERMS OF LAND AREA. BUT WYOMING IS THE LEAST POPULATED.

Together with her husband, she was awarded half of the Nobel Prize for Physics in 1903. In 1911 she received a second Nobel Prize, this time in Chemistry, in recognition of her work in radioactivity.

MARIE CURIE IS THE ONLY PERSON TO EARN A NOBEL PRIZE IN TWO DIFFERENT SCIENCES.

IN 2009, SCOTTISH SCIENTISTS SEARCHING FOR THE LOCH NESS MONSTER FOUND 100,000 GOLF BALLS INSTEAD.

MARTIN LUTHER KING, JR. GOT A C IN PUBLIC SPEAKING.

KOALAS HAVE FINGERPRINTS.

SEA LIONS CAN DANCE TO A BEAT.

There are only two mammals on Earth with the proven ability to move their bodies in time with an external beat: humans and sea lions.

IN FRANCE, IT'S ILLEGAL FOR EMPLOYERS TO SEND EMAILS AFTER WORK HOURS.

A FLIPPED COIN IS MORE LIKELY TO LAND ON THE SIDE IT STARTED ON.

JAM IS MADE
WITH MASHED-
UP FRUIT WHILE
JELLY IS MADE
WITH FRUIT JUICE.

PEANUT BUTTER CAN BE CONVERTED INTO DIAMONDS.

At around 3,000 degrees, and over five million pounds per square inch, the carbon bonds within the peanut butter will break down, allowing them to be reformed as diamonds.

THERE IS NO SPOT IN CENTRAL AMERICA MORE THAN 125 MILES FROM THE OCEAN.

WHEN SPLICED TOGETHER, THERE ARE 26 MINUTES OF QUIET STARING IN THE TWILIGHT FILM SERIES.

WIMBLEDON TENNIS BALLS ARE KEPT AT 68 DEGREES FAHRENHEIT.

YOU CAN SNEEZE FASTER THAN A CHEETAH CAN RUN.

A CATERPILLAR HAS MORE MUSCLES THAN A HUMAN.

A bite from the Lone Star tick can cause people to develop an allergy to red meat, including beef and pork. The Lone Star tick has been implicated in initiating the red meat allergy in the U.S., and this tick is found predominantly in the Southeast, from Texas to Iowa and into New England.

A TICK BITE CAN MAKE YOU ALLERGIC TO RED MEAT.

THE ORIGINAL FIRE HYDRANT PATENT WAS LOST IN A FIRE.

TOOTSIE ROLLS WERE USED AS PART OF THE RATIONS FOR WORLD WAR II SOLDIERS.

WATER CAN BOIL AND FREEZE AT THE SAME TIME.

ON GOOD FRIDAY IN 1930, THE BBC REPORTED, "THERE IS NO NEWS." INSTEAD, THEY PLAYED PIANO MUSIC.

Instead of a separate pouch where food collects, the platypus' esophagus is directly connected to its intestine.

THE PLATYPUS DOESN'T HAVE A STOMACH.

ELEPHANTS CAN'T JUMP.

Unlike those of most mammals, the bones in elephant legs are all pointed downwards, which means they don't have the "spring" required to push off the ground.

IN TENNESSEE, YOU CAN'T HOLD PUBLIC OFFICE IF YOU'VE BEEN IN A DUEL.

According to the Tennessee Constitution, it's illegal to hold public office if a person does any of the following: "fight a duel, or knowingly be the bearer of a challenge to fight a duel, or send or accept a challenge for that purpose, or be an aider or abettor in fighting a duel."

AN AA BATTERY WITH NO CHARGE REMAINING WILL BOUNCE WHEN DROPPED.

When dropped from an inch or two above a hard surface, a good battery won't bounce, and will sometimes land standing up. A dead battery, on the other hand, will bounce.

IT TAKES LIGHT FROM THE SUN EIGHT MINUTES TO REACH EARTH.

THE TINY POCKET IN JEANS WAS MADE FOR POCKET WATCHES.

FRANCE HAS A DOZEN TIME ZONES.

IT HAS BEEN ESTIMATED THAT ABOUT 500,000 PEOPLE AND OVER A MILLION WILD ANIMALS DIED IN THE ROMAN COLOSSEUM.

ASPARAGUS CAN GROW UP TO SEVEN INCHES IN A DAY.

OCEAN ALGAE PRODUCES ABOUT 70% OF THE WORLD'S OXYGEN.

EARTH WON'T ALWAYS HAVE THE SAME NORTH STAR.

Since it takes about 25,800 years for the Earth's axis to complete a single wobble, different stars have become the North Star at different times.

YOU BLINK OVER FOUR MILLION TIMES A YEAR.

A BALL OF GLASS WILL BOUNCE HIGHER THAN A BALL OF RUBBER OF THE SAME SIZE.

THE FIRST HOT AIR BALLOON PASSENGERS WERE A SHEEP, DUCK, AND ROOSTER.

On September 19, 1783 Pilatre De Rozier, a scientist, launched the first hot air balloon called "Aerostat Reveillon." The passengers were a sheep, a duck, and a rooster and the balloon stayed in the air for a total of 15 minutes before crashing back to the ground.

FLAMINGOS TURN PINK FROM EATING SHRIMP.

Flamingos are actually pink from eating algae that contains carotenoid pigments. Flamingos eat both algae and shrimp-like critters, and both contribute to their pinkness.

OYSTERS CAN CHANGE FROM ONE GENDER TO ANOTHER AND BACK AGAIN.

AFTER THE ATTACK ON PEARL HARBOR DURING WORLD WAR II, CANADA DECLARED WAR ON JAPAN BEFORE THE U.S. DID.

Four hours after Japan attacked Pearl Harbor, it attacked the British colony of Hong Kong, where Canada had troops. On hearing the news, Prime Minister MacKenzie King and his cabinet immediately decided to declare war on Japan. That was on the evening of December 7.

DISNEY WORLD IS 20 TIMES LARGER THAN DISNEYLAND.

THE TONGUE IS THE FASTEST-HEALING PART OF A HUMAN BODY.

This is due to the presence of saliva, which moisturizes the wound, improves immune response to wound healing, and contains other wound-healing promoting factors.

THE FIRST U.S. POSTAL STAMPS WERE ISSUED IN 1847.

THE FEELING OF GETTING LOST INSIDE A MALL IS KNOWN AS THE GRUEN TRANSFER.

The Gruen Transfer is caused by sensory overload and consequent confusion that puts people into some kind of a hypnotic trance. This is aided in malls by the shutting out of external distractions.

YOU ARE ALWAYS LOOKING AT YOUR NOSE: YOUR BRAIN JUST CHOOSES TO IGNORE IT.

THE CAESAR SALAD WAS BORN IN TIJUANA, MEXICO.

PEOPLE STARTED WEARING PAJAMAS INSTEAD OF NIGHTGOWNS SO THEY'D BE PREPARED TO RUN OUTSIDE IN PUBLIC DURING WORLD WAR I AIR RAIDS IN ENGLAND.

IN 1634, TULIP BULBS WERE A FORM OF CURRENCY IN HOLLAND.

In the 1600s the price of tulip bulbs in Holland soared. A single bulb could cost more than a house and in some cases tulip bulbs were used as a form of currency. Single bulbs would be sold multiple times, and investors would buy the rights to tulips yet to be grown. This created a futures market.

THE STARRY NIGHT DEPICTS VINCENT VAN GOGH'S VIEW FROM THE SAINT—PAUL DE MAUSOLE ASYLUM.

ADDING ALL OF THE NUMBERS ON A ROULETTE WHEEL WILL EQUAL 666.

THE POPSICLE WAS INVENTED IN 1905 BY AN 11–YEAR–OLD BOY.

Back in 1905, a San Francisco Bay Area kid by the name of Frank Epperson accidentally invented the summertime treat. He had mixed some sugary soda powder with water and left it out overnight. It was a cold night, and the mixture froze. In the morning, Epperson devoured the icy concoction, licking it off the wooden stirrer.

THE LIFESPAN OF A TASTE BUD IS ABOUT TEN DAYS.

THERE ARE MORE SAUNAS THAN CARS IN FINLAND.

HEAT, NOT SUNLIGHT, RIPENS TOMATOES.

Tomatoes don't need direct sunshine to ripen up; they only need warmth. You can bring a reddening tomato into the house and it will ripen on the counter. If you prune to open the tomatoes to sunshine and we get a sunny day, it can sunburn the tomatoes.

THERE'S A NIKOLA TESLA STATUE IN PALO ALTO THAT PROVIDES FREE WI-FI.

SUDAN HAS MORE PYRAMIDS THAN ANY COUNTRY IN THE WORLD.

Pyramids are well-known ancient Egyptian monuments, but what many people don't realize is that Sudan has more pyramids than Egypt. More than 200 pyramids were built in Sudan, as opposed to the 118 pyramids in all of Egypt, during the ancient reign.

THE LONGEST ATTACK OF HICCUPS LASTED 68 YEARS.

THE OFFICIAL STATE GEM OF WASHINGTON IS PETRIFIED WOOD.

A PELICAN CAN HOLD MORE FOOD IN ITS BEAK THAN ITS BELLY.

A GROUP OF JELLYFISH
IS CALLED A SMACK.

MONACO'S ORCHESTRA IS BIGGER THAN ITS ARMY.

THE WORD LIGHTSABER IS NEVER USED IN STAR WARS: EPISODE I.

THE U.S. GOVERNMENT GAVE INDIANA UNIVERSITY $1 MILLION TO STUDY MEMES.

MOST WASABI PASTE ISN'T REAL WASABI: IT'S HORSERADISH.

EACH YEAR, THE MOON MOVES AWAY FROM EARTH BY ABOUT FOUR CENTIMETERS.

As it moves away, its orbital period increases and Earth's rotation slows down. Looking at the average rate of retreat over the last four billion years, it should take about 50 billion years before the Moon takes as long to complete one orbit as Earth takes to complete one rotation.

AN ADULT WHITE RHINO CAN POOP AS MUCH AS 50 POUNDS PER DAY.

APART FROM VITAMIN C, EGGS CONTAIN EVERY SINGLE VITAMIN.

Eggs contain small amounts of almost every vitamin and mineral required by the human body, including calcium, iron, potassium, zinc, manganese, vitamin E, folate and many more.

A JIFFY IS AN ACTUAL UNIT OF TIME. IT'S 1/100TH OF A SECOND.

IF YOU SNEEZE WHILE DRIVING AT 60 MPH, YOUR EYES ARE CLOSED FOR AROUND 50 FEET.

BAMBOO GROWS SO FAST, IT'S MEASURED IN MILES PER HOUR.

CHICAGO IS NAMED AFTER SMELLY GARLIC THAT ONCE GREW IN THE AREA.

YOU CAN'T HUM IF YOU HOLD YOUR NOSE.

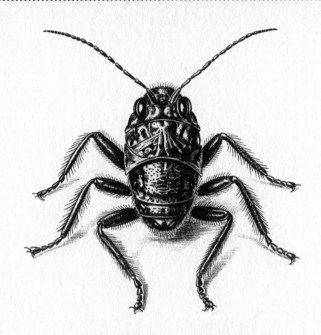

YOU CAN TELL
THE TEMPERATURE
BY COUNTING A
CRICKET'S CHIRPS.

Just count the number of chirps in 14 seconds, then add 40 to get the temperature. The number you get will be an approximation of the outside temperature.

CATS ONCE DELIVERED MAIL IN BELGIUM.

In the 1870s, the city of Liège, Belgium, attempted to employ 37 felines as mail carriers, according to the BBC. Messages were tucked into waterproof bags that the kitties would carry around their necks. However, while one cat apparently made it to its destination in under five hours, the other felines took up to a day to complete their journeys.

A STARFISH CAN TURN ITS STOMACH INSIDE OUT.

Oxytocin, a hormone commonly associated with love and bonding in humans, causes starfish to turn their stomachs inside out to feed. These findings provide vital new evidence for the evolutionary role of oxytocin and vasopressin neuropeptides as regulators of feeding in animals.

HAMARTOPHOBIA IS THE FEAR OF SINNING.

A MAN NAMED RONALD MACDONALD ONCE ROBBED A WENDY'S.

PICASSO BURNED MOST OF HIS EARLY WORK TO KEEP HIS APARTMENT WARM BECAUSE HE WAS POOR.

IN MANY ADVERTISEMENTS, THE TIME DISPLAYED ON A WATCH IS 10:10.

A DOLLAR BILL LASTS ROUGHLY 6.6 YEARS.

According to the Federal Reserve, the $1 bill has an average lifespan of 6.6 years, while the lifespan of a $100 bill is almost 23 years.

THE GUINNESS BOOK OF WORLD RECORDS WAS CREATED TO SETTLE BAR ARGUMENTS.

THE NAZIS DEVELOPED AN EXPERIMENTAL DRUG COCKTAIL NAMED D-IX. TEST SUBJECTS WHO HAD TAKEN IT COULD MARCH 55 MILES WITHOUT RESTING.

THE SPEED OF A COMPUTER MOUSE IS MEASURED IN "MICKEYS."

IN 2001, ARGENTINA HAD FIVE PRESIDENTS IN JUST TEN DAYS.

ALL THE ELECTRICITY POWERING THE INTERNET WEIGHS THE SAME AS AN APRICOT.

THE CROWN JEWELS CONTAIN THE TWO
BIGGEST CUT DIAMONDS ON EARTH.

A BLUE WHALE'S HEARTBEAT CAN BE DETECTED FROM UP TO TWO MILES AWAY.

But that's not the only interesting thing about a blue whale's heartbeat. On average, when it is at the surface of the water, the blue whale's heartbeat is around 25-35 beats per minute.

A BABY ECHIDNA IS CALLED A PUGGLE.

THE COST OF COLLEGE IN THE U.S. HAS GONE UP 500% SINCE 1985.

THE AVERAGE SNOWFLAKE FALLS AT ABOUT 3 MPH.

A GROUP OF BARRACUDAS IS CALLED A BATTERY.

THE AVERAGE PERSON WALKS THE EQUIVALENT OF FIVE TIMES AROUND THE WORLD THROUGHOUT THEIR LIFETIME.

ANCIENT EGYPTIANS USED TO WEAR HAIR EXTENSIONS.

As well as styling their own hair, the Egyptians also employed false hair. The earliest known example is a set of hair extensions from c. 3400 BC, discovered in a plundered female burial site at Hierakonpolis.

AN AVERAGE MAN WILL SPEND 145 DAYS OF HIS LIFE SHAVING.

AN OSTRICH'S EYE IS BIGGER THAN ITS BRAIN.

IT WOULD TAKE 19 MINUTES TO FALL FROM THE NORTH POLE TO EARTH'S CORE.

QUEEN ELIZABETH II OWNED MORE THAN 30 CORGIS.

LIGHTNING IS HOTTER THAN THE SURFACE OF THE SUN.

A return stroke of llightning—that is, a bolt shooting up from the ground to a cloud—can peak at 50,000 degrees Fahrenheit (F). The surface of the sun is around 11,000 degrees F.

IN A ROOM OF 23 PEOPLE,
THERE'S A BETTER—THAN—50%
CHANCE THAT TWO PEOPLE HAVE
THE SAME BIRTHDAY.

ON LAND, A TORTOISE CAN MOVE AS FAST AS 1 MPH.

A HIPPO'S JAW OPENS WIDE ENOUGH TO FIT A SPORTS CAR INSIDE.

DOGS WILL SOMETIMES FAKE BEING SICK TO GET ATTENTION.

THE U.S. AIR FORCE LOST A NUCLEAR BOMB SOMEWHERE OFF THE COAST OF GEORGIA.

GRIZZLY BEARS HAVE BEEN KNOWN TO COVER THEIR TRACKS.

Bears can remember hotspots for food even if it's been ten years since they last visited the area; some have been observed covering tracks or obscuring themselves with rocks and trees to avoid detection by hunters.

BABY CARROTS WERE INVENTED IN 1986.

GOLDFISH CAN DISTINGUISH THE MUSIC OF ONE COMPOSER FROM ANOTHER.

Scientists played four goldfish Bach's Toccata and Fugue in D Minor and Stravinsky's The Rite of Spring, training them to bite a red bead in their bowl when they heard the music. They were then trained to bite the bead to one piece and not the other and were able to identify the piece around three quarters of the time.

SIX GENERATIONS BACK, YOU HAVE 64 GREAT-GREAT-GREAT-GRANDPARENTS.

THERE IS AN OFFICIALLY RECOGNIZED SCHOOL OF WIZARDRY IN CALIFORNIA.

DUE TO THEIR EXTREME ATMOSPHERIC CONDITIONS, IT RAINS DIAMONDS ON NEPTUNE AND URANUS.

THERE ARE SPIDERS BIG ENOUGH TO EAT SNAKES IN AUSTRALIA.

THE SENTENCE "THE QUICK BROWN FOX JUMPS OVER A LAZY DOG" USES EVERY LETTER OF THE ALPHABET.

A FLOCK OF RAVENS IS CALLED AN UNKINDNESS.

IN WASHINGTON, IT'S ILLEGAL TO KILL BIGFOOT.

Bigfoot hunters, beware. Skamania County, Washington, passed a law in 1969 deeming the "slaying of Bigfoot to be a felony and punishable by 5 years in prison." The law was later amended, designating Bigfoot as an endangered species.

BEES CAN BE TRAINED TO DETECT BOMBS.

Bees learn to associate a particular smell with food, so that they automatically stick out their tongues. Honey bees are being trained to respond by sticking their tongues out when they sniff the aroma from explosives.

AN HOUR OF VACUUMING BURNS ABOUT 180 CALORIES.

FOUR IS THE ONLY NUMBER THAT HAS THE SAME AMOUNT OF LETTERS AS ITS ACTUAL VALUE.

IT TAKES ROUGHLY 40 GALLONS OF SAP TO MAKE 1 GALLON OF MAPLE SYRUP.

OUR BODIES CONTAIN ABOUT 0.2 MILLIGRAMS OF GOLD, MOST OF IT IN OUR BLOOD.

CATS CAN MAKE OVER 100 UNIQUE SOUNDS.

THE METAL BIT AT THE END OF A PENCIL THAT HOLDS THE ERASER IN PLACE IS CALLED A FERRULE.

SOMEONE WHO WEIGHS 150 POUNDS ON EARTH WOULD WEIGH 379.5 POUNDS ON JUPITER.

Anything and anyone will weigh 2.53 times on Jupiter what they do on Earth. Assuming you're actually able to find a place to stand on Jupiter, you would weigh about 2.53 times what you weigh on Earth. If you weigh 150 pounds on Earth, for example, you would weigh 379.5 pounds on Jupiter.

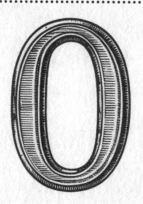 ANCIENT GREEKS AND ROMANS DIDN'T HAVE A NUMBER FOR ZERO.

DUNCE CAPS USED TO BE SIGNS OF INTELLIGENCE.

Thirteenth-century philosopher John Duns Scotus believed that a pointed cap would help spread knowledge from the tip to the brain, and his "Dunsmen" followers wore them as a badge of honor.

FIGS AREN'T CONSIDERED VEGAN BECAUSE THEY HAVE DEAD WASPS INSIDE.

THERE'S A FRUIT THAT TASTES LIKE CHOCOLATE PUDDING.

The black sapote is a species of persimmon often referred to as the "chocolate pudding fruit." This is because the flavor, texture and appearance of the fruit resembles a dense chocolate mousse.

THE WORLD'S FIRST MOVIE THEATER OPENED IN LOS ANGELES IN 1902.

HEADPHONES CAN INCREASE THE BACTERIA IN YOUR EARS.

CAT URINE GLOWS UNDER A BLACK LIGHT.

AUSTRALIA IS WIDER THAN THE MOON.

THE REAL NAME FOR A HASHTAG IS AN OCTOTHORPE.

THE MOON HAS MOONQUAKES.

Moonquakes are produced as a result of meteoroids hitting the surface or by the gravitational pull of the Earth squeezing and stretching the Moon's interior, in a similar way to the Moon's tidal pull on Earth's oceans.

THE AUSTRALIAN GOVERNMENT BANNED THE WORD "MATE" FOR A DAY.

In 2005, Australian Parliament took a few citizen complaints a little too seriously and banned anyone on their staff from using the word "mate" while at work. Fortunately, Prime Minister John Howard objected, claiming that "mate" was an important part of Australian culture and the ban was overturned within 24 hours.

TORNADOES CAN CAUSE "FISH RAIN."

THERE'S AN ENTIRE TOWN UNDER A ROCK.

SAUDI ARABIA IMPORTS CAMELS FROM AUSTRALIA.

SWEAT DOESN'T ACTUALLY STINK.

SHARKS CAN LIVE FOR ALMOST FOUR CENTURIES.

Greenland Sharks are known to be some of the oldest living animals in our world. Researchers did carbon dating on a Greenland Shark that was caught in 2014 and found it to be around 392 years old.

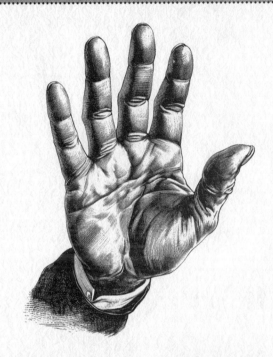

GOODBYE COMES FROM THE PHRASE GOD BE WITH YE.

PUFFINS MATE FOR LIFE.

It is widely believed that puffins mate for life although they do not begin the mating process until age five. When nesting, female puffins lay just one egg per breeding year with an incubation period of 42 days. Puffins make their homes in crevices between rocks or use their webbed feet to dig burrows.

AN OLIVE TREE CAN LIVE UP TO 1,500 YEARS.

The oldest known olive tree is 1,500 years old, but the average life span is 500 years. Olive trees are loved for their fruits, eaten fresh or brined and pressed into oil. But not all olive trees bear olives.

WOMEN OWN ABOUT 40% OF ALL BUSINESSES IN THE U.S.

THE PROBABILITY OF YOU BEING BORN WAS ABOUT ONE IN 400 TRILLION.

WHEN FRUIT FLIES ARE INFECTED WITH A PARASITE, THEY SELF-MEDICATE WITH ALCOHOL.

THERE IS AN ESTIMATED $60 BILLION IN SUNKEN TREASURE SITTING AT THE BOTTOM OF THE WORLD'S OCEANS.

ALBERT EINSTEIN DIDN'T SPEAK IN FULL SENTENCES UNTIL THE AGE OF 9.

FOR EVERY THREE MILLION PEOPLE ON EARTH, THERE IS ONE BILLIONAIRE.

EARTHWORMS ARE HERMAPHRODITES.

MODERN HORSES HAVE LOST THEIR ADDITIONAL TOES.

The distant ancestors of modern horses had hooved toes instead of a single hoof, which vanished over time, according to researchers.

CARROTS WERE ORIGINALLY PURPLE.

WINSTON CHURCHILL'S MOTHER WAS BORN IN BROOKLYN.

Winston Churchill's roots were British and American. He was uniquely placed to stand up for the shared values of freedom and liberty so nearly lost in those dark days of 1940. His mother, Jennie Jerome, was born in Brooklyn in 1854.

NOT A SINGLE ENGINEER
SURVIVED THE TITANIC.

They stayed on board to keep the power going so other passengers could escape. The Chief Engineer, Joseph Bell, is briefly depicted in the 1997 film Titanic heating some soup on a boiler plate (which he and others were known to do) and responding to the evasive orders from the ship's bridge when the iceberg was sighted.

THE AVERAGE U.S. WORKER STAYS AT EACH JOB FOR 4.4 YEARS.

STAYING AWAKE FOR TWO WEEKS STRAIGHT CAN KILL YOU.

DOLPHINS ARE UNABLE TO SMELL.

MARILYN MONROE HAD A HIGHER IQ (163) THAN THAT OF ALBERT EINSTEIN (160).

KIT KATS ARE CONSIDERED GOOD LUCK IN JAPAN.

PINEAPPLES ARE NOT A SINGLE FRUIT, BUT A GROUP OF BERRIES THAT HAVE FUSED TOGETHER.

A pineapple is neither a pine nor an apple, but a fruit consisting of many berries that have grown together.

PISTACHIOS CAN SPONTANEOUSLY COMBUST.

The popular mid-afternoon treat has a tendency to generate heat on its own if packed in large quantities due to its high levels of fat and low water content. The fats in pistachios can break down through reactions with the air as the nut decomposes.

THE SPACE BETWEEN YOUR EYEBROWS IS CALLED THE "GLABELLA."

IF YOU HEAT UP A MAGNET, IT WILL LOSE SOME OF ITS MAGNETISM.

ON AVERAGE, A 4-YEAR-OLD CHILD ASKS 437 QUESTIONS A DAY.

BLUE FLAMES ARE THE HOTTEST, REACHING TEMPS UP TO 3,000 DEGREES CELSIUS.

LIONS CANNOT ROAR UNTIL THEY REACH THE AGE OF ONE.

Male lion cubs cannot roar and instead make a purring sound. This is to avoid alerting prey that danger may be close. Female cubs are able to roar within a few months beyond one year of age.

IN UTAH, BIRDS HAVE
THE RIGHT OF WAY
ON THE HIGHWAY.

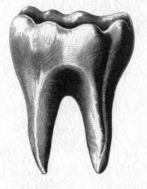

A RAT CAN FALL FROM A FIVE— STOREY BUILDING WITHOUT INJURIES.

AN ADULT HUMAN HAS 32 TEETH.

THE WORLD'S SMALLEST WASP IS SMALLER THAN AN AMOEBA.

IF YOU WERE TO PRODUCE A SOUND LOUDER THAN 1,100 DB, YOU WOULD CREATE A BLACK HOLE AND DESTROY THE GALAXY.

THE FIRST BREAKFAST CEREAL HAD TO BE SOAKED OVERNIGHT BEFORE IT COULD BE EATEN.

EXPLORER FERDINAND MAGELLAN NAMED THE PACIFIC OCEAN IN THE 16TH CENTURY.

"HUH?" IS UNDERSTOOD IN ALL LANGUAGES.

KETCHUP USED TO BE SOLD AS MEDICINE.

In the 1830s, tomato ketchup used to be sold as a medicine, claiming to cure ailments like diarrhea, indigestion, and jaundice. The idea was first proposed by Dr. John Cook Bennett, an American physician, in 1834, who is said to have sold the recipe later in the form of "tomato pills."

YOU CAN BUY A FLYING BICYCLE.

THE LONGEST WALKING DISTANCE IN THE WORLD IS 14,000 MILES.

Stretching 14,000 miles from Cape Town in South Africa to Magadan in Russia, this route might be the world's longest walk, and it certainly sounds grueling.

MCDONALD'S INTRODUCED ITS DRIVE—THROUGH SERVICE DUE TO THE MILITARY.

IKEA RUGS WERE USED FOR THE NIGHT'S WATCH CLOAKS IN GAME OF THRONES.

A U.S. PARK RANGER ONCE GOT HIT BY LIGHTNING SEVEN TIMES.

Roy Cleveland Sullivan (February 7, 1912 – September 28, 1983) was an American park ranger in Shenandoah National Park in Virginia. Between 1942 and 1977, Sullivan was claimed to have been struck by lightning on seven occasions, surviving all of them.

A SHARK IS THE ONLY KNOWN FISH THAT CAN BLINK WITH BOTH EYES.

All sharks have eyelids, but they serve more as a defense against injuries than to keep the water out of their eyes or to keep their eyes clean. Many species, including tiger sharks and hammerhead sharks, have a third eyelid called a nictitating membrane that allows them to blink their eyes.

AN EGYPTIAN CITY WAS DISCOVERED UNDERWATER IN 2013 AFTER BEING LOST FOR 1,200 YEARS IN THE MEDITERRANEAN SEA.

Thonis-Heracleion was left relatively undisturbed beneath the sea floor for 1,200 years. Sand and other debris covered the remains of the city and made accidental discovery unlikely. This kept Thonis-Heracleion preserved.

EATING WATERMELON CAN REDUCE BLOOD PRESSURE.

THE ORIGINAL NAME FOR THE BUTTERFLY WAS "FLUTTERBY."

THE WORLD'S LARGEST FALAFEL WEIGHED 223 POUNDS.

63 EARTHS COULD FIT INSIDE URANUS.

A 26-SIDED SHAPE IS KNOWN AS A SMALL RHOMBICUBOCTAHEDRON.

LAMBORGHINI CARS WERE INVENTED WHEN THE LAMBORGHINI TRACTOR COMPANY WAS INSULTED BY THE CREATOR OF FERRARI.

TOMATOES AND CUCUMBERS ARE FRUITS.

THE FAMILIAR SMELL OF RAIN IS CALLED PETRICHOR.

OXFORD UNIVERSITY IS OLDER THAN THE AZTEC EMPIRE.

VENUSTRAPHOBIA IS THE FEAR OF BEAUTIFUL WOMEN.

Most men love attractive women, but in the case of some individuals, the very thought of seeing a beautiful woman, let alone speaking to her, can cause a full-blown panic attack.

LEMONS FLOAT,
BUT LIMES SINK.

Limes are a little denser than lemons—not by much, but the difference is just enough to cause them to sink in liquid.

IN 30 MINUTES, THE HUMAN BODY
GIVES OFF ENOUGH HEAT TO BRING
A GALLON OF WATER TO A BOIL.

ON MARS, SUNSETS ARE BLUE.

THE AVERAGE AMERICAN TYPICALLY EATS BETWEEN 3,000 AND 5,000 CALORIES AT THANKSGIVING DINNER.

THE WORLD'S OLDEST OPERATING LIBRARY IS IN MOROCCO.

ENGLAND IS HIT WITH MORE TORNADOES PER SQUARE MILE THAN ANY OTHER COUNTRY IN THE WORLD.

BUZZ ALDRIN LEFT A COPY OF PLAYBOY ON THE MOON.

MODERN BRUNCH WAS FIRST PROPOSED IN 1895 AS A POST-HANGOVER MEAL.

PIRATES WORE EARRINGS BECAUSE THEY BELIEVED IT IMPROVED THEIR EYESIGHT.

Without any science behind this rumor, the widely held belief among the pirate community was that the precious metals forming the earring had magic powers to heal their vision.

IN 2006, AN AUSTRALIAN ATTEMPTED TO SELL NEW ZEALAND ON EBAY.

36 HUMAN HEARTS COULD FIT INSIDE A GIRAFFE'S HEART.

FOUR BILLION YEARS FROM NOW, OUR GALAXY, THE MILKY WAY, WILL COLLIDE WITH OUR LARGE SPIRALED NEIGHBOR, ANDROMEDA.

WATER BOTTLE EXPIRATION DATES ARE FOR THE BOTTLE, NOT THE WATER.

SERVING ICE CREAM ON CHERRY PIE IN KANSAS WAS PROHIBITED.

Kansans don't mess around with their cherry pie. At one point, it was illegal in the state to top a slice of cherry pie with a scoop of ice cream. According to the Kansas Secretary of State, it's unclear how this law originated or whether it's still technically on the books, but—fortunately for dessert lovers—it's not enforced.

NUTMEG IS A HALLUCINOGEN.

Consumption of nutmeg seeds in large quantities causes a hallucinogenic effect, which is followed by unpleasant side effects such as facial flushing, tachycardia, hypertension, dry mouth, feelings of euphoria, unreality, and delirium.

THE FIRST FAX MACHINE WAS PATENTED IN 1843.

A GROUP OF FROGS IS CALLED AN ARMY.

AT BIRTH, A BABY PANDA IS SMALLER THAN A MOUSE.

CLAMS CAN LIVE FOR MORE THAN 500 YEARS.

THE WORLD'S FIRST ANIMATED MOVIE WAS MADE IN ARGENTINA.

THE SPIRAL SHAPES OF SUNFLOWERS FOLLOW THE FIBONACCI SEQUENCE.

NEPHOPHOBIA IS THE FEAR OF CLOUDS.

IT TAKES ABOUT SEVEN MINUTES FOR THE AVERAGE PERSON TO FALL ASLEEP.

GERMAN CHOCOLATE CAKE WAS INVENTED IN TEXAS.

RAIN CONTAINS VITAMIN B12.

DR. SEUSS WROTE GREEN EGGS AND HAM AS PART OF A BET.

FLOWERS CAN GROW FASTER BY LISTENING TO MUSIC.

Believe it or not, studies indicate that plants also seem to have a specific taste in music! Some genres of music promote growth, whereas others can be damaging. Roses in particular seem to love violin music. For most plants playing classical or jazz music caused growth to increase, while harsher metal music induced stress.

COMPETITIVE ART WAS ONCE AN OLYMPIC SPORT.

From 1912 to 1948, artists could earn medals for painting, music, sculpture, and even architecture.

BRITISH MILITARY TANKS ARE EQUIPPED TO MAKE TEA.

British tanks come equipped with a "boiling vessel" that, as you can imagine, is commonly used to brew up a cup of tea during the tank's downtime.

NASA USES COUNTDOWNS BECAUSE OF A SCI—FI FILM.

The countdown Fritz Lang used to create suspense in the rocket launch scene of his 1929 silent film Frau im Mond didn't just change film history—it also inspired NASA to use countdowns before its own blastoffs. It's not exactly a race against the clock though. NASA can feel free to pause the clock to check mechanical difficulties.

A NARWHAL'S TUSK REVEALS ITS PAST LIVING CONDITIONS.

GOOSEBUMPS ARE MEANT TO WARD OFF PREDATORS.

Goosebumps caused our ancestors to appear bigger than they were, helping to ward off predators when they were frightened or on the defense. With modern humans having less body hair, goosebumps no longer cause us to look that much more intimidating.

DANES ONCE BRED A PIG TO LOOK LIKE THE FLAG.

THERE'S A DEVICE THAT CREATES ENERGY FROM SNOWFALL.

THE FIRST COMPUTER WAS INVENTED IN THE 1940S.

In the U.S., in 1940 Arthur Dickinson (IBM) invented the first digital electronic computer.

THE LONGEST WEDDING VEIL WAS THE SAME LENGTH AS 63.5 FOOTBALL FIELDS.

CHEWING GUM BOOSTS CONCENTRATION.

ONLY TWO MAMMALS LIKE SPICY FOOD: HUMANS AND THE TREE SHREW.

SUPERMAN DIDN'T ALWAYS FLY.

BEES SOMETIMES STING OTHER BEES.

In protecting their hives from outsiders, some "guard bees" will stay by the entrance and sniff the bees that come in. If there's a rogue bee from another hive trying to steal some nectar, the guard bee will bite and even sting the intruder.

THE EIFFEL TOWER
WAS SUPPOSED TO
BE IN BARCELONA.

When Gustave Eiffel's design was rejected by the Spanish city for being too ugly, he pitched it to France. The locals weren't in love with it either, but tourists from around the world flock to Paris to see it!

SOME SEA SNAKES CAN BREATHE THROUGH THEIR SKIN.

This happens thanks to arteries containing much lower oxygen concentrations than the surrounding seawater, which allows oxygen to diffuse through the skin and into the blood.

YOU LOSE UP TO 30% OF YOUR TASTE BUDS DURING FLIGHT.

The elevation in an airplane can have a detrimental effect on our ability to taste things. According to a 2010 study conducted by Germany's Fraunhofer Institute for Building Physics, the dryness experienced at a high elevation as well as low pressure reduces the sensitivity of a person's taste buds to sweet and salty foods by about 30%.

THE WOOD FROG CAN HOLD ITS PEE FOR UP TO EIGHT MONTHS.

YOUR NOSTRILS WORK ONE AT A TIME.

HUMANS ARE THE ONLY ANIMALS THAT BLUSH.

PINEAPPLE WORKS AS A NATURAL MEAT TENDERIZER.

DOLPHINS HAVE BEEN TRAINED TO BE USED IN WARS.

BEE HUMMINGBIRDS ARE SO SMALL THEY GET MISTAKEN FOR INSECTS.

THE HEALTHIEST PLACE IN THE WORLD IS IN PANAMA.

CHILDREN'S MEDICINE ONCE CONTAINED MORPHINE.

PRO BASEBALL ONCE HAD WOMEN PLAYERS.

RIDING A ROLLER COASTER COULD HELP YOU PASS A KIDNEY STONE.

SOME PEOPLE HAVE AN EXTRA BONE IN THEIR KNEE.

It turns out that some people have a bone in their knee called a fabella. And while this particular little bone with an unknown purpose was once fading away, over the last century and a half, it's gotten more common.

A DOZEN BODIES WERE ONCE FOUND IN BENJAMIN FRANKLIN'S BASEMENT.

Multiple skeletons were discovered during a 1998 renovation of the house and were identified as being from nearly a dozen people, including six children. The most plausible explanation is not mass murder, but an anatomy school run by Franklin's young friend and protege, William Hewson.

A PHARAOH ONCE LATHERED HIS SLAVES IN HONEY TO KEEP BUGS AWAY FROM HIM.

King Pepi II thought so highly of himself that when he was bothered by insects, he would command that one of his slaves be covered in honey to lure the flies away from himself.

PLASTIC EASTER EGGS WERE INVENTED BY A MAN WHO HOLDS MORE PATENTS THAN THOMAS EDISON.

If you've ever enjoyed an Easter basket with plastic eggs and grass, then you can thank Donald Weder, the man who invented both. Weder not only holds the patents on these holiday staples, he also holds a total of 1,413 U.S. patents.

THE LEGEND OF THE LOCH NESS MONSTER GOES BACK NEARLY 1,500 YEARS.

CHINESE POLICE USE GEESE SQUADS.

FOR 100 YEARS, MAPS HAVE SHOWN AN ISLAND THAT DOESN'T EXIST.

TYPHOID MARY INFECTED MORE THAN 50 PEOPLE BY COOKING FOR THEM.

ROLLS-ROYCE MAKES THE MOST EXPENSIVE CAR IN THE WORLD.

A KOALA'S BRAIN IS ONLY 0.2% OF ITS BODY WEIGHT.

In addition, the koala's brain is quite smooth and not folded like in most animals (and humans), which means there's less room for brain cells.

ABOUT 159,635 PEOPLE WILL DIE ON THE SAME DAY AS YOU.

THE PINEBERRY IS A WHITE STRAWBERRY THAT TASTES LIKE A PINEAPPLE.

IF YOU DROP SILLY PUTTY FROM A GREAT HEIGHT, IT'LL SHATTER INSTEAD OF BOUNCE.

THE LIGHTER WAS INVENTED BEFORE THE MATCH.

ABRAHAM LINCOLN'S BODYGUARD LEFT HIS POST AT FORD'S THEATRE TO GO FOR A DRINK.

John Frederick Parker was both Lincoln's bodyguard and the guy drinking with John Wilkes Booth next door at the Star Saloon minutes before Booth left to kill Lincoln.

PLAYING THE ACCORDION WAS ONCE REQUIRED FOR TEACHERS IN NORTH KOREA.

The most popular instrument in North Korea is the accordion, so much so that all teachers used to be required to play to get their teaching certifications. Because the accordion is portable in a way that, say, a grand piano isn't, it was thought of as the "people's instrument" that could be taken outside and played for laborers in the fields.

IT IS ILLEGAL TO SELL A "BOUNCELESS" PICKLE TO SOMEBODY IN CONNECTICUT.

The law was in fact an ordinance that was created in 1945 to thwart pickle packers Moses Dexler and Sidney Sparer. These two men were selling inedible pickles, so laboratories conducted experiments and found that if it doesn't bounce, don't eat an ounce!

THE WORD "HIPSTER" GOES ALL THE WAY BACK TO THE 1930S.

THERE'S AN ENTIRE FAMILY IN ITALY THAT FEELS ALMOST NO PAIN.

IN GERMANY, PEOPLE HELP TOADS CROSS THE ROAD.

ONE MAN ONCE SURVIVED TWO ATOMIC BOMBS.

Tsutomu Yamaguchi survived both nuclear attacks on Japan when the U.S. dropped atomic bombs during World War II. Yamaguchi, sent to Hiroshima on business on August 6, 1945, saw the U.S. drop the first atomic bomb. Miraculously, he survived with burns across his face and arms, but made it home to Nagasaki. Three days later, the second atomic bomb hit, flattening Yamaguchi's home.

BEETHOVEN COULD STILL HEAR AFTER GOING DEAF.

Upon going deaf, Beethoven discovered that if he bit onto a metal pole that connected to the piano he was playing, he could hear almost perfectly well.

THE MOST-HIGHLIGHTED BOOK ON AMAZON IS A SELF-HELP BOOK.

GERMANY UNCOVERS 2,000 TONS OF UNEXPLODED BOMBS EVERY YEAR.

ONE MAN WAS ONCE CONSTIPATED FOR NEARLY TWO MONTHS.

THE SILVERBACK GORILLA CAN LIFT ALMOST A LITERAL TON.

The Silverback gorilla can lift up to 10 times its body weight on average: a total of about 1,800 pounds, according to the Guinness Book of World Records.

HUMANS AREN'T THE ONLY SPECIES TO ADOPT.

THERE ARE NO MUSCLES IN YOUR FINGERS.

The muscles that move the finger joints are in the palm and forearm. The long tendons that deliver motion from the forearm muscles may be observed to move under the skin at the wrist and on the back of the hand.

SOME SEA CUCUMBERS FIGHT WITH THEIR GUTS.

When threatened, they'll shoot out their internal organs, which are poisonous to predators. They'll sometimes get rid of their entire digestive systems but the organs grow back.

SCIENTISTS WERE ABLE TO TAKE A PICTURE OF AN ATOM'S SHADOW.

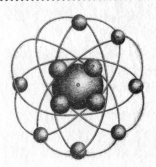

THE BRITISH ROYAL FAMILY IS NAMED AFTER WINDSOR CASTLE.

THE WORLD'S LARGEST WATERFALL IS UNDERWATER.

SHADOWS ARE DARKER ON THE MOON.

MAINE IS THE ONLY STATE THAT BORDERS JUST ONE OTHER STATE.

If you're in Maine, you'll find the Atlantic Ocean to the south and Canada to the north. But if you want to stay in the U.S., you'll have to head west to New Hampshire, because Maine is the only state in the country that borders just one other state.

YOU CAN RENT OUT AN ENTIRE COUNTRY.

For just $70,000 you can rent Lichtenstein for an evening. If that seems excessive, you can always just rent one of the six Austrian villages, three German towns, or one Swiss ski-resort village.

YODA AND MISS PIGGY WERE VOICED BY THE SAME PERSON.

THE LAS VEGAS STRIP ISN'T IN LAS VEGAS.

ALASKA IS BOTH THE WESTERNMOST AND EASTERNMOST STATE IN THE UNITED STATES.

OPHIDIOPHOBIA IS THE FEAR OF SNAKES.

YOU CAN HEAR RHUBARB GROWING.

Rhubarb doesn't get a lot of love but the stalky plant does have an amazing talent: It grows so fast you can actually hear it.

THERE'S AN ANT SPECIES
THAT'S UNIQUE TO
NEW YORK CITY.

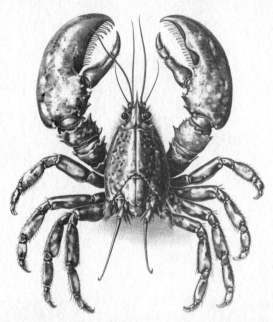

LOBSTERS TASTE WITH THEIR FEET.

Tiny bristles inside a lobster's little pincers are their equivalent to human taste buds. Meanwhile, lobsters' teeth are in one of their three stomachs.

KING CHARLES HAS A CAR FUELED BY WINE.

In the search for more efficient fuels, King Charles is taking a strange but entertaining approach: The British King had his vintage Aston Martin reworked to use wine as its primary fuel.

AN AUSTRALIAN LAKE IS NATURALLY BUBBLEGUM PINK.

THE MODERN KEYBOARD WAS DESIGNED TO MAKE PEOPLE TYPE SLOWER.

MOST CANADIANS LIVE SOUTH OF SEATTLE.

THE U.S. GOVERNMENT HAS AN OFFICIAL PLAN FOR A ZOMBIE APOCALYPSE.

THERE IS A COUNTRY WITH NO CAPITAL.

Nauru is the only country in the world without an official capital city. The government offices of the tiny Pacific island nation are located in the Yaren District.

EVENTUALLY, A DAY ON EARTH WILL BE 25 HOURS LONG.

The Earth's speed as it orbits the sun is not a fixed rate. No matter how constant it may seem to us mortals, it's actually slowing over time. The length of a day will become 25 hours in about 175 million years.

THE CITY OF LONDON ONLY HAS A POPULATION OF 9,000.

SESAME SEEDS WERE ONCE WORTH MORE THAN GOLD.

VINCENT VAN GOGH ONLY SOLD ONE PAINTING IN HIS LIFETIME.

THE LARGEST DESERT IN THE WORLD IS COVERED IN SNOW.

THE LARGEST PADLOCK IN THE WORLD WEIGHS 916 POUNDS.

The largest padlock in the world was created by a team of students and teachers at Russia's Pavlovo Arts College and measures 56.8 inches tall, 41.3 inches wide, and 10.2 inches deep.

MICHELANGELO WROTE A POEM ABOUT HOW MUCH HE HATED PAINTING THE SISTINE CHAPEL.

One translation of the poem he sent to his friend begins: "I've already grown a goitre from this torture, hunched up here like a cat in Lombardy (or anywhere else where the stagnant water's poison)." Doesn't sound like he was too thrilled with his task.

POLAR BEARS AREN'T WHITE, THEY'RE JUST GLOWING.

When sunlight hits the bear, it undergoes a complex scattering process within the fur, with a small amount of light eventually being reflected. Since the sun's light is white, it's the color we perceive polar bears to be.

"BANANA" FLAVORING IS BASED ON AN EXTINCT TYPE OF BANANA.

This variety of banana was the standard in America until the 1950s, when a fungus essentially wiped out the Gros Michel. The milder-tasting Cavendish replaced the Gros Michel as our go-to banana.

AFTER A KIDNEY TRANSPLANT. YOU ACTUALLY HAVE THREE KIDNEYS.

AMERICA'S FIRST BANK ROBBER DEPOSITED THE MONEY BACK INTO THE SAME BANK.

THE WORLD'S DEADLIEST CREATURE CAN BE CRUSHED BETWEEN YOUR THUMB AND FOREFINGER.

Mosquitoes—more specifically, the diseases carried by mosquitoes – kill nearly 1 million people every year. The main culprit is Malaria, a disease that may be responsible for killing up to half of all the people who have ever lived.

ABOUT 0.5% OF PEOPLE ALIVE TODAY ARE DESCENDED FROM GENGHIS KHAN.

Genghis Khan is known for being one of the most prolific killers ever but it appears he was just as much a lover as he was a fighter. Recent DNA analysis found that about 0.5% of all men alive today are his descendants.

THERE'S A MOUNTAIN SO TALL ON MARS THAT YOU WOULDN'T KNOW IT WAS THERE IF YOU WERE STANDING ON TOP OF IT.

THE RAPTOR SOUNDS IN JURASSIC PARK ARE ACTUALLY MATING TORTOISES.

DRUG LORD PABLO ESCOBAR SPENT $2,500 A MONTH ON RUBBER BANDS TO HOLD ALL HIS CASH.

It can be hard to imagine how much wealth is generated by the illegal drug trade but the fact that Pablo Escobar had to spend over two grand on rubber bands every month just to keep his money together might help put it in perspective.

THE INSCRIPTION ON THE ONE RING IN LORD OF THE RINGS ISN'T ELVISH.

EVERY TWO MINUTES PEOPLE TAKE
MORE PHOTOS THAN WERE TAKEN
IN THE ENTIRE 19TH CENTURY.

IT'S TOTALLY LEGAL TO ESCAPE FROM PRISON IN SOME COUNTRIES.

In Belgium, Germany, the Netherlands, Sweden, Austria and other countries, the philosophy of the law holds that it is human nature to want to escape. In those countries, escapees who do not break any other laws are not charged and no extra time is added to their sentence (except time may be added by suspended parole).

PISTOL SHRIMP CAN MAKE A SOUND LOUDER THAN A GUN AND KILL PREY USING BUBBLES.

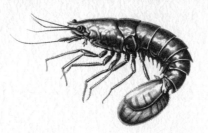

THE MONGOLIAN NAVY CONSISTS OF ONE SMALL TUGBOAT AND SEVEN MEN.

TWO OUT OF EVERY THREE EMAILS SENT ARE SPAM.

THE OWNER OF SEGWAY WAS KILLED BY A SEGWAY.

TOM AND JERRY WERE ORIGINALLY NAMED JASPER AND JINX.

A WAR WAS STARTED BY A SOCCER GAME.

In 1969, the soccer teams of Honduras and El Salvador were competing for a spot in the 1970 World Cup. Tensions mounted as the teams were tied 1-1 and went into a third match. When El Salvador won the play-off, riots erupted. The riots boiled over into a full-scale war with over 2,000 casualties on each side. After four days of fighting, the 100 Hour War was ended.

SOURCES

P4. https://www.washingtonpost.com/lifestyle/style/handshake-greeting-germs-elbow-bump/2020/05/15/e341acb6-9465-11ea-91d7-cf4423d47683_story.html

P6. https://www.cam.ac.uk/research/news/how-sloths-got-their-long-neck

P8. https://www.scientificamerican.com/article/this-sea-slug-can-chop-off-its-head-and-grow-an-entire-new-body-twice1/

P9. https://www.beautyanswered.com/is-lipstick-made-from-fish-scales.htm

P10. https://www.burkemuseum.org/collections-and-research/biology/herpetology/all-about-amphibians/all-about-frogs

P12. https://www.snopes.com/fact-check/mermaids-the-body-found/

P13. https://whatculture.com/offbeat/20-weird-science-facts-that-you-might-just-need-one-day?page=10

P13. https://www.nobelprize.org/prizes/physics/1903/marie-curie/facts/

P14. https://www.pinterest.com/pin/863424559799433795/

P16. https://indianapublicmedia.org/amomentofscience/peanut-butter-diamonds.php

P17. https://acaai.org/allergies/allergic-conditions/food/meat/

P18. https://www.thedodo.com/the-improbable-platypus-7-fact-668223014.html

P19. https://www.science.org/content/article/elephants-can-t-jump-and-here-s-why

P20. https://tennesseeencyclopedia.net/entries/dueling/

P21. https://www.mcgill.ca/oss/article/did-you-know-general-science/do-dead-batteries-really-bounce-and-charged-ones-not

P22. https://www.space.com/15567-north-star-polaris.html

P23. https://balloonfiesta.com/Hot-Air-History

P24. https://reidparkzoo.org/blog/what-makes-flamingos-pink/

P25. https://www.warmuseum.ca/war-against-japan/

P25. https://homework.study.com/explanation/what-is-the-fastest-healing-organ-in-the-human-body.html

P26. https://en.wikipedia.org/wiki/Gruen_transfer

P27. https://www.spokesman.com/stories/2017/may/14/in-the-17th-century-tulip-bulb-mania-created-the-w/

P29. https://www.npr.org/sections/thesalt/2015/07/22/425294957/how-an-11-year-old-boy-invented-the-popsicle

P29. https://www.seattletimes.com/life/lifestyle/tomatoes-need-warmth-not-direct-sunlight-to-ripen/

P30. https://punchng.com/did-you-know-sudan-has-more-pyramids-than-egypt/

P33. https://www.astronomy.com/science/ask-astro-how-quickly-is-the-moon-moving-away-from-earth/

P34. https://www.healthline.com/nutrition/6-reasons-why-eggs-are-the-healthiest-food-on-the-planet

P35. https://www.loc.gov/everyday-mysteries/meteorology-climatology/item/can-you-tell-the-temperature-by-listening-to-the-chirping-of-a-cricket/

P36. https://theculturetrip.com/europe/belgium/articles/cats-used-to-deliver-the-news-in-this-belgian-city/

P37. https://neurosciencenews.com/oxytocin-starfish-14622/

P38. https://www.federalreserve.gov/faqs/how-long-is-the-life-span-of-us-paper-money.htm

P40. https://www.practically.com/web/blog/do-you-know-that-a-blue-whales-heart-beats-just-twice-a-minute.php

P42. https://intarch.ac.uk/journal/issue42/6/3.cfm

P43. https://www.weather.gov/safety/lightning-temperature

P45. https://www.mentalfloss.com/article/531450/facts-about-grizzly-bears

P46. https://www.classicfm.com/composers/bach/news/goldfish-can-recognise-classical-music/

P48. https://www.kuow.org/stories/did-you-know-why-you-shouldn-t-mess-with-bigfoot-in-washington-state

P49. https://en.wikipedia.org/wiki/Hymenoptera_training

P50. https://a-z-animals.com/blog/this-is-how-much-youd-weigh-on-jupiter/

P51. https://www.shortpedia.com/en-in/funny-facts/fun-facts-about-humans/fun-fact-dunce-caps-used-to-be-signs-of-intelligence-1650265664

P53. https://www.thestar.com.my/news/true-or-not/2022/12/06/quickcheck-is-there-a-fruit-that-tastes-like-a-chocolate-dessert

P53. https://www.nasa.gov/press-release/goddard/2019/moonquakes/

P54. https://apnews.com/article/d3de9b39c6e7066fb69842f470997d2d

P54. https://www.reuters.com/article/us-science-shark/long-in-the-tooth-the-greenland-shark-may-live-four-centuries-idUSKCN10M208

P56. https://www.maine.gov/sos/kids/about/wildlife/puffin

P57. https://ucanr.edu/blogs/blogcore/postdetail.cfm?postnum=44360

P58. https://www.eurekalert.org/news-releases/992976

P59. https://www.britannica.com/biography/Jennie-Jerome-Churchill

P60. https://www.quora.com/Is-it-true-that-not-a-single-engineer-of-Titanic-survived

P61. https://www.lovebigisland.com/quick-and-remarkable-facts-about-hawaii/pineapple/

P62. https://www.tastingtable.com/850505/do-pistachios-actually-combust/

P63. https://rangerplanet.com/facts-about-lions/

P66. https://htschool.hindustantimes.com/editorsdesk/knowledge-vine/tomato-ketchup-the-condiment-that-was-once-used-as-a-medicine

P66. https://www.popularmechanics.com/science/a30285283/longest-walkable-distance-earth/

P67. https://news.yahoo.com/roy-sullivan-struck-lightning-seven-101301879.html

P68. https://animalvivid.com/do-sharks-have-eyelids/

P69. https://en.wikipedia.org/wiki/Heracleion

P70. https://exploringyourmind.com/venustraphobia-the-fear-of-beautiful-women/

P71. https://www.bestfoodfacts.org/lemons-float-limes-sink/

P74. https://www.optimax.co.uk/blog/pirates-believe-earrings-improved-eyesight/

P75. https://www.usatoday.com/list/news/nation-now/weirdest-laws-every-state/53ad0541-3518-4432-adc4-0fec193d389e/

P76. https://en.wikipedia.org/wiki/Myristicin

P78. https://pistilsnursery.com/blogs/journal/music-and-plant-growth-heres-what-the-science-says

P79. https://en.wikipedia.org/wiki/Art_competitions_at_the_Summer_Olympics

P80. https://coffeeordie.com/british-tea-tanks

P81. https://www.the-sun.com/tech/6254077/strange-reason-nasa-countdown-clock-popular-movie/

P81. https://www.awpnow.com/main/2022/03/11/goosebumps-are-meant-to-ward-off-predators/

P82. https://en.wikipedia.org/wiki/History_of_computing_hardware

P82. https://www.buzzaboutbees.net/can-bees-sting-other-bees.html

P83. https://www.rd.com/list/eiffel-tower-facts/

P84. https://www.adelaide.edu.au/research/news/list/2019/09/04/deep-breath-this-sea-snake-gathers-oxygen-through-its-forehead

P85. https://www.vernonmorningstar.com/news/morning-start-you-lose-up-to-30-of-your-taste-buds-during-flight/

P86. https://royalsociety.org/science-events-and-lectures/2023/07/do-you-have-extra-bones/

P87. https://www.smithsonianmag.com/smart-news/why-was-benjamin-franklins-basement-filled-with-skeletons-524521/

P88. https://face2faceafrica.com/article/pepi-ii-the-egyptian-king-who-covered-naked-slaves-with-honey-to-attract-flies-away-from-him

P89. https://www.smithsonianmag.com/innovation/thank-one-americas-most-prolific-inventors-hinged-plastic-easter-egg-180971972/

P90. https://www.factslides.com/i-3892

P91. https://www.washingtonpost.com/history/2021/05/02/lincoln-missing-bodyguard-assassination/

P92. https://commonplacefacts.com/2019/08/29/reading-writing-and-accordions-education-in-north-korea/

P93. https://ifunny.co/picture/did-you-know-it-is-illegal-to-sell-a-bounceless-FwjibAh07

P93. https://www.history.com/news/the-man-who-survived-two-atomic-bombs

P94. https://www.classicfm.com/composers/beethoven/guides/deaf-hearing-loss-composing/

P94. https://phcorner.net/threads/the-silverback-gorilla-can-lift-almost-a-literal-ton.1734430/

P97. https://en.wikipedia.org/wiki/Evisceration_(autotomy)

P97. https://en.wikipedia.org/wiki/Maine

P98. https://www.wired.co.uk/article/liechtenstein-airbnb

P98. https://www.americastestkitchen.com/cooksillustrated/articles/3075-the-best-rhubarb-grows-in-the-dark

P100. https://www.grunge.com/1207082/why-lobsters-cant-taste-food-without-their-feet/

P101. https://www.foodandwine.com/king-charles-aston-martin-runs-on-cheese-and-wine-7496349

P101. https://htschool.hindustantimes.com/editorsdesk/knowledge-vine/nauru-the-pleasant-island-without-a-capital

P102. https://www.pbs.org/wgbh/nova/article/in-200-million-years-days-will-be-25-hours-long/

P102. https://ke.opera.news/ke/en/culture/78a788b04eacd933d7ce7402fc3b4241

P103. https://www.mentalfloss.com/article/651560/michelangelo-poem-about-sistine-chapel

P104. https://snowbrains.com/polar-bears-fur-not-white/

P105. https://www.americastestkitchen.com/articles/3952-the-reason-artificial-banana-flavor-tastes-nothing-like-real-bananas

P105. https://www.si.edu/sidedoor/ep-3-worlds-deadliest-animal

P106. https://www.nationalgeographic.com/culture/article/mongolia-genghis-khan-dna

P106. https://www.businessinsider.com/pablo-escobar-and-rubber-bands-2015-9

P108. https://en.wikipedia.org/wiki/Prison_escape

P109. https://www.bbc.com/news/world-latin-america-48673853